MW00422798

Finding Peace in an Anxious World

By Rev. Mark Flynn

All Scripture passages are from the New International Version.

Table of Contents

Introduction - The Idea

This is not a self-help book. I do not claim to have discovered a simple three step process by which you can cast anxiety out of your life forever. Although Americans spend enormous amounts of money on such cure-alls, we know they don't work. If they did, none of us would have nervous stomachs or tense shoulders, and sleepless nights would be a thing of the past. If there were a quick and easy path to peace, our culture would not be filled with enormous stress about the state of the world and our own future.

Let me clarify, when speaking of anxiety and stress, I am not referring to clinical depression or anxiety disorders. People who suffer from these medical conditions need our support and encouragement on their difficult journey, but they also need to be under a physician's care. This book is aimed at the general anxiety which has been steadily growing over the last fifty years to the point that now it affects almost everyone in our culture.

In his book, *My Age of Anxiety*, Scott Stossel notes that only three academic papers were published on anxiety in 1927. By 1941, that number had increased to fourteen, and by 1950, it had grown to thirty-seven. Today, physicians report that anxiety is one of the most common complaints of their patients. If you perform even a cursory internet search, you will discover millions of articles on the subject of what causes our anxiety.

Please note that when we talk about "causes" of anxiety, we do not mean the events or trends that rightly cause reasonable people concerns: terrorism, economic downturns, unemployment, widespread social transformation, etc. These are very real issues, and we should take them seriously, but they are not the cause of our anxiety. People can be informed on these issues, understand their potential impact, and allow their presence to influence decision making without becoming filled with general anxiety about that which has not yet actually impacted their lives. However, these circumstances and tragic news provide the fodder that feeds our fears. The more we dwell on the possibility, however remote, of their potential destructive power, the more stress we bear waiting on those possible horrors to arrive. So, the "causes" of anxiety refers to how we respond to events.

As is often the case regarding questions of why we feel, think, or act as we do, there is no consensus on the exact reason stress is such a modern phenomenon. However, I find there are common threads among those writing about the causes of the widespread anxiety found in our culture. The seven topics which arise most often suggest anxiety is a result of:

* receiving an overabundance of negative information,
* linking our value as a human being to achievement,
* feeling alone, while continually connected to social media for fear of missing out on something important,
* living in increasing isolation from one another,
* feeling helpless,
* refusing to accept negative feelings as a normal part of life, and
* feeling hopeless about the future.

I'm no expert in psychology or sociology, but these make sense to me. I believe most of us can see how these seven "forces" are at work in the modern world. I am also aware the Bible has something to say regarding these causes of anxiety.

So, we will examine some of the biblical passages which address these topics. How have faithful people dealt with stress? What did Jesus model for us as he dealt with anxiety, especially as he prepared for and endured the cross.

If you have any questions about what you are reading, any comments you want to share, feel free to call me at 423-892-9363 or email me at pastor@christchurchchatt.org.

May the God of hope
fill you with all joy and peace
as you trust in him,
so that you may overflow with hope
by the power of the Holy Spirit.
Romans 15:13

Chapter One - Focus on Good News

My wife, Annette, and I have many things in common. We are both United Methodist ministers. We both love listening to classical music - classic rock, that is. And hot buffalo wings are easily our favorite food. However, no relationship is without its differences, and ours is no exception. One of those differences is apparent every evening in our home. Annette likes to watch the local television news; I do not.

Don't get me wrong, I want to stay informed. It is just that I prefer to read the newspaper, listen to the radio, or glance over an online newsfeed. For years I couldn't understand why listening to newscasts in the car or scrolling through headlines does not bother me but watching the six o'clock news drives me crazy. Then, it hit me: it is the visuals.

Each of those information sources has its own strengths and weaknesses. For instance, newspapers usually provide a large number of background details with each story. The people who produce television news know the strength of their medium is video footage. Nobody wants to watch news anchors read all the details available in a newspaper. What "viewers" want is visuals. So, producers send reporters and videographers out to locations around our city to capture shots of tragedy unfolding, the aftermath of devastation, and people grieving or celebrating - and, of course, lots of weather maps swirling with colors.

I don't mind the weather reports, although I have to wonder "why do we need the same information packaged fifteen different ways in thirty minutes?" No, the clever weekly forecasts don't annoy me. It is the video of one tragic scene after another.

I am a visual person. Or, better said, I can't un-see things. If I read a headline about a house fire or listen to a report on war devastating a region, I can retain the information without feeling emotionally overwhelmed by events over which I have no control. If I see someone grieving the loss of their home or a hospital filled with battle casualties, I immediately feel anxious, even though the suffering is not my own. I intellectually know there is nothing I can do to help them, but

I continue to feel the negative emotions tied to the visuals of those who are suffering.

I realize not everyone thinks like this. We are all uniquely wired creatures. But regardless of whether you are more inclined to feel stress sitting over a newspaper splashed with headlines or a Facebook page crawling with people arguing politics, studies show that one reason modern people suffer anxiety (even during times of peace and relative prosperity) is that news sources rely on negative information to drive viewership.

Not too long ago I watched a local news report about a propane tank that exploded behind someone's house. I don't remember the reason; the reporter didn't focus on what went wrong. What I remember is how quickly the newscast turned to how many propane tanks there were in America and how each of these were ticking time bombs of destruction. The report led viewers by the hand from one local explosion to suggest a devastating crisis is at hand.

I don't honestly know if we prefer to hear bad news, have been conditioned to believe tragedy is more pertinent to our lives, or just like to watch other people's dirty laundry in order to feel superior. People offer each of these as the reason negative news sources receive higher ratings. Most likely the issues are far more complex than we can grasp.

However, regardless of why we lean into bad news, the reality is that it affects how we live. We are an anxious people and it feels as if we live in a world teetering on an abyss where any minute something horrible might happen. We need to find a way to stay engaged with the realities of the world without feeling overwhelmed. We need peace in the midst of an anxious world.

Gaining a Balanced View

That brings us to a very touchy subject. I do not want anyone to think that I am ignoring the concerns and tragedies that engulf our world. Terrorism is real. Gang violence is devastating our communities. The world's current lifestyle is perpetrating serious environmental damage on the earth. We all know that those who can afford expensive lawyers do not go to jail for the same crimes that send the poor to prison. The list goes on, but....

...there is also an amazing amount of good news about life in the world today.

You would never know it from news broadcasts, but we are currently living in an amazingly positive era where violence in the world is on the decline. Yes, random acts of violence and shootings are horrible and grab headlines, but those highly publicized actions do not change the positive trends in violence and war around the world. I heard a radio report last week on how a study from the Brennan Center for Justice at the NYU School of Law indicates crime rates are down from last year and half what they were in 1990. Data also shows there is increasing widespread support for women's right and a decline in violence against women. Democracy is on the rise; autocracy on the decline. The under-five mortality rate has declined by nearly half (49%) since 1990. Under-five mortality is falling faster than at any other time during the past two decades. Disease and pestilence is on the decline.

Take a look in the bibliography for a few of the numerous articles on these and other positive trends.

Ideally, we would hear both the good and bad news of the world. We would read about how people are living longer, but the rate of nonfatal diseases and injuries is increasing – that is what happens when more people grow old! How wonderful if we had a balanced diet of positive and negative news, but we do not. For whatever reason, bad news gets higher ratings, and advertisers pay for the highest possible ratings....and we are left with the feeling that the world is barely staying afloat.

What would happen if we gained a more balanced view of life, if we began to focus more of our attention on the positives in the world? What might happen if we focused on good news for a change? Isn't it interesting the Bible describes Jesus' teaching as the "good news?" (Mark 1:15)

Where Do We Focus?

There are well over 300 scripture passages which address anxiety. The longest of these is a part of the "sermon on the mount," which recounts an extended teaching of Jesus before a large crowd. He addresses the issue of worry and concludes by teaching us where to focus our attention.

"Therefore I tell you, do not worry about your life, what you will eat or drink; or about your body, what you will wear. Is not life more than food, and the body more than clothes? Look at the birds of the air; they do not sow or reap or store away in barns, and yet your heavenly Father feeds them. Are you not much more valuable than they? Can any one of you by worrying add a single hour to your life? And why do you worry about clothes? See how the flowers of the field grow. They do not labor or spin. Yet I tell you that not even Solomon in all his splendor was dressed like one of these. If that is how God clothes the grass of the field, which is here today and tomorrow is thrown into the fire, will he not much more clothe you—you of little faith? So do not worry, saying, 'What shall we eat?' or 'What shall we drink?' or 'What shall we wear?' For the pagans run after all these things, and your heavenly Father knows that you need them.

But seek first his kingdom and his righteousness, and all these things will be given to you as well." (Matthew 6:25-34)

Jesus knows us. Human beings spend an amazing amount of energy worrying about life in general, food, drink, clothing, and future security. He is not saying that these essentials do not matter. Unlike many ascetics of his day, he did not teach to eat and drink as little as possible. Remember, he was accused by some people of being a glutton and a drunk (Matthew 11:16-19).

The question is "on what do we focus?" If we spend our time and energy worrying about having enough, we end up missing the gift that brings abundance to our life. Jesus instructs us to seek God first rather than worry. If we focus on God and God's kingdom (God's way of living, God's desires for us and the creation), we find the flipside of worry: peace.

Jesus teaches this same lesson when he is asked which of the 613 commandments found in the Jewish Law is the greatest. *"The most important one,"* answered Jesus, *"is this: 'Hear, O Israel: The Lord our God, the Lord is one. Love the Lord your*

*God with all your heart and with all your soul and with all your
mind and with all your strength.' The second is this: 'Love your
neighbor as yourself.' There is no commandment greater than
these."* (Mark 12:29-31)

Loving God is what matters most. And the amazing part is that
keeping our Creator at the center of our attention does not
mean we become fanatics, ignoring reality or the needs of
people around us. Loving God is tied to loving others. When
our priority is to focus on God, then we are compelled to love
those God loves.

Unfortunately, Jesus was not able to convince everyone to
hear his "good news" that God's kingdom is here in our midst.
He knew that some people are so addicted to bad news, so
engulfed with how terrible the world is, that they cannot
accept the idea that a loving God exists and desires to bring
them a life of abundance.

Many people have memorized John 3:16 over the years: *"For
God so loved the world that he gave his one and only Son, that
whoever believes in him shall not perish but have eternal life."*

Fewer have taken the time to study the next verse: *"For God did not send his Son into the world to condemn the world, but to save the world through him."* Even fewer make their way down to verse 19 of that passage: *"This is the verdict: Light has come into the world, but people loved darkness instead of light…"* God desires us to discover light even when we are in the dark places of the world. But we do not always embrace the gift being offered.

In using the metaphor of light, Jesus is actually drawing on a long tradition in scripture. God's first recorded act is bringing light into darkness (Genesis 1:1-4). From the beginning, faithful people have made a connection between the light of God and overcoming anxiety.

The LORD is my light and my salvation—
    whom shall I fear?
The LORD is the stronghold of my life—
    of whom shall I be afraid? (Psalm 27:1)

A good first step in dealing with the widespread anxiety of our culture is to recognize that we have an unbalanced perception of the world. We have given too much of our time to hearing bad news and not enough of our attention to the light God offers, to the good news found in the world and Jesus' teachings.

You will keep in perfect peace
  those whose minds are steadfast,
  because they trust in you.
Trust in the LORD forever,
  for the LORD, the LORD himself, is the Rock eternal.
(Isaiah 26:3-4)

Light of the World

So, how do we get connected to the light of God? What can we do to trust God more and find that kind of peace?

As I said in the Introduction, this is not a self-help book. Finding peace will take more than reading seven uplifting truths, even if they are in the Bible. However, (are you ready for a big leap not everyone seems to understand?) the goal of scripture is not to teach us intellectual ideas about God, Jesus, or ourselves. The Bible tells us the history of the Jewish people (in the Old Testament) and the early Church (in the New Testament) so that we will have a personal encounter with God ourselves. Jesus came to teach us a new way to live. One of the most important aspects of that new life is that God's Spirit is present and available to us.

Even though electricity is available in most homes, we have to plug into an outlet to take advantage of its presence. If we want to experience the "light of God," then we need to connect with the Spirit of God that is present in the world.

Every Thursday night, Annette and I go on a date. We make time for that because it matters to us. We try to spend time together, even if it is for just a few moments, every day. If one of us is traveling, we talk on the phone. We don't have a perfect marriage, but intentionally talking together every day reminds us that we are not alone in the world. Staying connected to the Spirit and experiencing the presence of God is no different - it requires purposely setting aside time each day to make a connection. The way you connect with God's

Spirit may be a little different from how I connect. After all, not everyone enjoys the hot buffalo wings Annette and I share.

Followers of Jesus have a term for the many ways they find for spending time with God: spiritual practices.

Our ability to feel God's presence, to trust God, and to find the peace of God in the midst of difficult circumstances is linked to our spending time with God. This makes perfect sense considering the first part of this chapter: what we focus on matters.

But don't worry - I'm not talking about spending hours and hours each day chanting or in monastic silence.

A Spiritual Practice

For each of the seven anxiety-inducing topics, we will learn about one spiritual practice to connect with God's peace. Find the practices that work for you. There is no "one size fits all" method of relaxing into the presence of God. In order to move beyond talking about peace and, instead, experience God's presence, we need to intentionally invest in our spiritual life.

The spiritual practice which helps us find a healthy balance of good and bad news involves creating Sabbath time. Most of us associate "Sabbath" with setting aside one day a week to worship God with other believers. Scripture does emphasize the importance of weekly communal worship. But as a spiritual practice, Sabbath is a broader concept. It concerns more than going to church; it is about finding an unforced, healthy rhythm for our life.

Our spirits need time for rest, just like our bodies. If we don't sleep for long periods of time, our ability to think and function suffers. Lack of sleep can make emotions swing wildly out of control and even produce paranoia. Well, the reverse is also true: if we do not set aside time to spiritually recharge, our physical and emotional selves are wounded. Sleep is a natural part of a healthy life - so is spiritual rest.

Set aside time each day to rest your soul. (Some say "to feed your hungry soul." Which metaphor makes sense to you?) You probably have an idea about how best to do this. There are as many different ways as there are people. Some of us need to sit quietly and become aware of God's presence. Others need an activity (walking, painting, gardening, listening to music) to relax and reflect on God's good gifts. Be willing to try something new to find what works for you.

Likewise, for some, setting aside fifteen minutes a day for rest and reflection is adequate. After that, our souls feel nourished and ready to go. For others, three hours may not be enough. Again, nobody can give you the one, perfect answer for what Sabbath will mean for you. It is like our taste in food. You, and only you, can know what tastes good to you, what causes an allergic reaction, and when you are full. Invest some time to know how much Sabbath rest you need.

If you are like me, you need to plan today when you will set aside time to rest tomorrow. If I am not intentional, the day's responsibilities and my habits push me along until I find myself in bed dozing off - not exactly the quality time and attention God deserves.

The Bible does emphasize the importance of including communal worship in the rhythm of each week. Regular worship enables us to explore how best to love God and our neighbors. Find a community of faith that supports, inspires, and encourages you to become the person you were created to be.

Above all, give yourself a break from bad news. Make the effort to see the beauty of the creation and share time with friends. And don't forget: all of us need to hear God's good news regularly. Find an unforced, restful rhythm in your life. You may want to consider stepping away from your phone or computer for a time...but more about that in the next chapter.

Remember God is with you and invites you to find Sabbath. Your Creator says, *"be still, and know that I am God."* (Psalm 46:10)

Chapter Two - Learn Who You Are

According to sociologists who measure stress levels around the world, the United States is the most anxious country on earth. Even nations where people have difficulty meeting basic physical needs, like clean water and adequate food, are noticeably less anxious than Americans. According to the 2002 World Mental Health Survey, folks in developing-world countries are up to five times less likely to show clinically significant anxiety levels than Americans.

I believe most of us know, or at least suspect, the reason why this is true. The American dream is not to have clean water and enough food to eat. We are bombarded with the message that more is better than less, and new is better than old. Wall Street, Madison Avenue, and the neighbors next door who just bought a new car all seem to convey the same idea: more new stuff will makes us happy.

I was one of those people who refused for a long time to get a smart phone. My old "Juke" flip phone was easily over ten years old and the size of a pocket knife. I liked how small it was, and the curmudgeon in me loved being able to sneer, "I don't need a phone to do anything except make calls." Whenever a student saw me take it out to make a call, they thought it must be a new, hip style. I loved that.

Then my beloved phone broke. I went to a store to pick out another anti-smart phone, but I made the mistake of listening to the salesperson. "Yes, it would be nice to have photos of my grandchildren right here. Why yes, having access to my full "rolodex" (those under 25 years old may need to look up that word) would be helpful. What do you mean it cost less than a dumb phone!?" And then it happened. I had a vision of how this new phone would make my life easier and more content. I bought the phone, the data plan, and a protective case! (Something so valuable must be kept safe!)

Now I have **more**. The photos of my grandkids are great and having my contacts is nice. But now I also have "more" opportunities to work, no matter where I am. Between the constant pull of email, texts, games, and a web browser that lets me explore the world, I have more distractions from the people standing right in front of me. The salesman forgot to mention that more doesn't mean better. But, then again, I knew that in the back of my mind even as I was flirting with buying the thing.

We know the fairy tale isn't true - at least all the new, shiny things we purchased in the past didn't bring lasting contentment. When we feel like something IS missing, we are tempted to believe that maybe this time the happiness will linger a little longer. So we strive for more: a perfect home, greater income, a better job, the perfect body...whatever is being touted as the next great cure for feeling inadequate.

The promise of more happiness for us and our loved ones always hangs just out beyond our grasp. The myth which links contentment and **more** together drives one of our most basic anxieties: I am only as valuable as my level of achievement in the world.

If I am convinced my peace of mind will increase when my home is perfect, then I will measure my achievement as a home-maker against the beauty and coziness of home magazines and staged photos on Pinterest. Automobiles, Bible knowledge, children's grades, baking ability, video games, athletic prowess - whatever we decide matters in life will become the yardstick of achievement we use to decide if we are successful.

Let's also be honest enough to admit we do not compare ourselves to average people. If that were the case, our home, car, and grades might look just fine. We compare ourselves to the best of the best. We examine our bank account in light of Bill Gates' wealth. We look in a mirror and think about air-brushed and coiffed models. In other words, we determine our value by measuring what we can accomplish, produce, or earn in comparison to the highest achievers. We know this is absurd, but everyone does it. Where can we find a different understanding of our value?

Finding a New Perspective

"Humility" is one of our most misunderstood words. Most people define "humility" as not thinking too highly of oneself or putting our natural gifts and abilities in a negative light so as not to appear proud. Sadly, that definition has become standard in our culture, but it is not the traditional meaning of the word. And it is certainly not the biblical one.

According to Scripture, humility means knowing who we are in the presence of God (the victories, failures, talents, temptations, strengths, weaknesses). At first glance, this might sound like a terrible idea. After all, if we get depressed comparing ourselves to celebrities and tycoons, how will we fare standing next to God!?

But, ironically, the reverse is actually true. When we stand in the presence of God, we discover that, yes, our self-centeredness is clearly visible, but so are our God-given gifts. To spend time in honest confession of sin (as absolutely necessary as that step is) is to discover the light of love and forgiveness offered in Jesus Christ. Those who allow God's light into their lives find a new perspective on themselves and their blessings. God does not want us to wallow in our failures any more than we want that same misery for people we love. God desires us to move from confession to new life!

To recognize that our sins do not ultimately define us, to experience the joy of being accepted right where we are, to know we can leave those failures behind and live as the beloved children of God we are created to be, THAT is a joyful, liberating moment where we can discover peace.

Your True Identity

Writing to the Church, Peter understands that humility, knowing who you really are, is the basis for discovering peace. He describes humility not only in terms of overcoming pride but discovering God's love.

"All of you, clothe yourselves with humility toward one another, because, "God opposes the proud but shows favor to the humble." Humble yourselves, therefore, under God's mighty hand, that he may lift you up in due time. Cast all your anxiety on him because he cares for you."
(1 Peter 5:6-7)

"Humble yourselves..." Find opportunities to reflect on who you are in the presence of God. Be honest about everything:

sins, blessings, fears, gifts, abilities, and doubts. Your abilities are to be celebrated! False humility demands that you feel badly about your talents, but once we understand God blesses us with physical and mental abilities, we can be grateful for our gifts and seek to use them "with humility toward one another."

If my self-esteem depends on believing myself superior to others, I have a problem. I have to overlook my own issues and find fault with you. That is why pride breaks down friendships and undermines community. Do you know people who constantly criticize others? As hard as it is to believe, they are demonstrating just how insecure they are. What a horrible way to treat others. We do not have to live this way (Galatians 6:4-6).

Your true identity is found in your connection with God. Your value is not elevated when you are covered in jewels or surrounded by trophies. You are a child of God. Your value is not diminished if you are out of work or homeless. You are a child of God. The world did not give you that identity and cannot take it away from you. You are of infinite worth because of whose you are. When we dispel the myth that our value is tied to achievement then we can stop striving to be someone we are not. We are comfortable regardless of what we find ourselves doing.

That is why Jesus does not mind acting as a servant for others. He knows who he is regardless of the circumstances. He is the Messiah whether acknowledged by the world or not. He is the Lord when he is being served or washing someone's feet.

"When he had finished washing their feet, he put on his clothes and returned to his place. 'Do you understand what I have done for you?' he asked them. 'You call me "Teacher" and "Lord," and rightly so, for that is what I am. Now that I, your Lord and Teacher, have washed your feet, you also should wash one another's feet. I have set you an example that you should do as I have done for you. Very truly I tell you, no servant is greater than his master, nor is a messenger greater than the one who sent him. Now that you know these things, you will be blessed if you do them." (John 13:12-17)

Anyone who believes they are "too good" to care for others is actually trying to convince themselves they are valuable. They are driven by the fear they are unimportant. How sad - they do not realize they are beloved children of God. What is worse is that any goal they do achieve reminds them that something is still missing from their life. So they redouble their efforts in order to feel good about themselves. That drive to prove one's worth by continually achieving more in order to feel superior to others helps create the anxiety that characterizes the American desire for more.

Peter's advice is to *"humble yourselves...under God's mighty hand, that he may lift you up in due time."* The goal of acknowledging who you are in God's presence is to raise you up! *"Cast all your anxiety on him because he cares for you."* God desires to carry the burdens under which you have been struggling. God desires for you to find rest by remembering you are a beloved child, and nobody can ever take that true identity away from you. Discover the peace that comes from remembering who God is and who you are.

A Spiritual Practice

There are many spiritual practices which might help us calm and quiet ourselves in God's presence. Certain types of prayer play this role for many people. However, I think a very ancient practice called "divine reading" is a wonderful tool for reflecting on our relationship with God. Known to many by its Latin name "Lectio Divina," this way of reading and reflecting on scripture goes back to the 3rd century.

Most of the time, our goal in reading scripture is to understand the context of the biblical passage so we can learn its general meaning. The goal of divine reading is quite different. It is to allow God's Spirit to speak personally to us. This practice invites us to treat scripture as a living Word that can connect us with the living God.

There are four steps in this sort of reading: reading, meditation, prayer, contemplation.

1) Quiet your heart and mind as much as possible and slowly read a short passage. This first reading helps us get into the

right frame of mind. Next, ask God to use the biblical words to reveal to you what you need to hear in that moment. Then, read the passage again, looking (listening, becoming aware - what verb makes the most sense to you?) for what God might be saying to you. 2) Sit for as long as necessary, meditating on the passage, allowing it to lead your thoughts. 3) When the time feels right, spend a little time in prayer, both speaking to God about what you are hearing (or not hearing) and actively listening with all your senses to what God might be saying to you. 4) Finally, when you have relaxed enough into the text to feel the calm of Spirit's presence, slowly read the passage one final time, and sit in silence, aware of the God's love for you.

This practice can be used on any passage of scripture. For many people over the centuries, this meditating on scripture provided the foundation for their spiritual life. If you are interested in giving divine reading a try, I would suggest you begin with one of the readings in this chapter: 1 Peter 5:6-7, John 13:12-17, or Psalm 131.

Or, here is one other passage to consider. Take your time. Relax. Consider giving divine reading a chance.

"At that time the disciples came to Jesus and asked, 'Who, then, is the greatest in the kingdom of heaven?' He called a little child to him, and placed the child among them. And he said: 'Truly I tell you, unless you change and become like little children, you will never enter the kingdom of heaven. Therefore, whoever takes the lowly position of this child is the greatest in the kingdom of heaven'." (Matthew 18:1-4)

Chapter Three - Stay Connected

Before we explore the next cause of anxiety, I want to encourage you to not give up. Finding peace requires putting in some effort and being patient with yourself.

Learning to relax into the presence of God requires finding that natural, healthy rhythm and spiritual practices that work for you. Countless people can attest to the fact that it is possible, but it is not always easy. Embracing peace is like developing a healthy lifestyle. Reading about exercise and eating well is much easier than putting up with sore muscles and ignoring those potato chip cravings. The same is true when it comes to finding peace.

Don't be surprised if your attempts at Sabbath time are interrupted by unruly thoughts or family responsibilities. Few people experience a relaxed peace the first time they try divine reading. After all, most of us have to train our mind to rest. Do not give into worries that you are not "spiritual" enough. You are fine. Each of us is unique, and we have to find the spiritual practices that work for us.

Likewise, you may feel the first two causes of anxiety (an overabundance of negative information and tying value to achievement) are not what is driving your personal stress. If that is the case for you, wonderful. Continue to be open as we examine a few other possibilities. Do not settle for a life that is less than the abundance God desires for you (John 10:10). As Paul so often writes in the introductions to his letters to the Church, "Grace and peace to you from God our Father and the Lord Jesus Christ." (Ephesians 1:2)

Paul assumes, like so many other writers in the Bible, that both grace (unearned love) and peace are a result of a positive, ongoing connection to God. That assumption is one of the first lessons we are taught in scripture. The first chapters of Genesis, the first book of the Bible, teach many things, but among the most important is that humanity is made in God's image (Genesis 1:27).

There are lots of interpretations of what it means to be made "in the image of God." It does not mean we physically look like God. Until Jesus comes, God is spirit, not flesh (John 4:24). Some people believe that being made in God's image means having a moral sensibility - we know right from wrong. Others claim it suggests we are creative, as God is creative. After all, in the next verse God says, "be fruitful and multiply."

Whether being made in the image of God means either or both of these things, there is one interpretation of these verses that everyone agrees upon: humans are created to be connected with God and one another.

According to those first chapters of Genesis, we are made to be in positive relationships with both God and other people. We will examine our need for community in Chapter Four. However, whenever you read scripture, you will find that most writers assume that relationships with God and fellow Christians are essential and intertwined. For example, when

Paul writes to followers of Jesus in the city of Philippi, he emphasizes the importance of both.

"Therefore, my brothers and sisters, you whom I love and long for, my joy and crown, stand firm in the Lord in this way, dear friends! I plead with Euodia and I plead with Syntyche to be of the same mind in the Lord. Yes, and I ask you, my true companion, help these women since they have contended at my side in the cause of the gospel, along with Clement and the rest of my co-workers, whose names are in the book of life.

"Rejoice in the Lord always. I will say it again: Rejoice! Let your gentleness be evident to all. The Lord is near. Do not be anxious about anything, but in every situation, by prayer and petition, with thanksgiving, present your requests to God. And the peace of God, which transcends all understanding, will guard your hearts and your minds in Christ Jesus.

"Finally, brothers and sisters, whatever is true, whatever is noble, whatever is right, whatever is pure, whatever is lovely, whatever is admirable - if anything is excellent or praiseworthy - think about such things. Whatever you have learned or

received or heard from me, or seen in me - put it into practice. And the God of peace will be with you." (Philippians 4:1-9)

We could have read those last few verses in Chapter One's discussion of focusing on good news - think about what is right, pure, lovely, and admirable. But for now, let's consider Paul's suggestion to deal with anxiety through prayer. This is not a naïve belief that repeating a few magic words about God's protection will keep harm away. We must remember that Paul wrote these words from a jail cell! His twenty years of work is under attack, and he is tired (Philippians 1:12-26). So, when he encourages us not to be anxious about anything, he is not speaking flippantly.

He is talking about maintaining a life of prayer. His phrase "in every situation," reminds me of similar advice in another of his letters. *"Rejoice always, pray continually, give thanks in all circumstances; for this is God's will for you in Christ Jesus."* (1 Thessalonians 5:16-18)

Anyone with common sense understands that Paul does not expect followers of Jesus to spend twenty four hours a day with head bowed and eyes closed. He is using "prayer" in a broader sense. Prayer is about becoming aware of God's presence and guidance regardless of the circumstance.

The realization that God is with us changes how we interact with people, how we deal with frustration, and how we handle stressful situations. Just as having a few friends at our side makes a difference in how we face the day, when our connection with God is secure, the ups and downs of life are put into a new perspective. Unfortunately, not everyone has a strong awareness of the divine.

There may be occasions when we savor being alone, but nobody enjoys being lonely. We are made in the image of God. We long to connect with our Creator. When we do not feel a connection with God, we look to those around us to fulfill that longing. Opportunities to communicate with people all over the world are a hallmark of modern life! We have unprecedented access to our friends and family. We have evolved from the days of expensive long distance telephone calls to a world wide web offering online "community" and social media "friends."

However, the gift of modern communication has not solved all our interpersonal problems. Supportive friendships are a gift of God, but the sad reality is that our drive to be in relationship is so strong that if healthy relationships are not available, we will settle for unhealthy ones.

Fear of Missing Our Connection

This is not a rant about the evils of modern technology. Far from it! It is an acknowledgement that we can take any good gift a little too far. Long before parents complained their children were incessantly texting their friends, teens were being accused of tying up the family's "land line," calling at ungodly hours. It should be noted, however, that my parents would have never used that particular term, and my dad's idea of an ungodly hour was any time after 9 p.m.

With every good cultural advancement comes a temptation to abuse it. When I was young, I was warned countless times about watching too much television and sitting too close to the luxurious 14 inch screen. We have advanced technologically, but our tendency to overindulge remains the same.

We all have friends who are addicted to checking their phones. Most of us have experienced sitting around a dinner table only to discover everyone staring at their phone or tablet instead of talking to each other. It does not surprise us to learn that one of the causes of anxiety for many people is related to this felt need to be constantly connected at all times.

Dr. Heather Cleland Woods and Holly Scott of the University of Glasgow have studied the connection between the impact of social media on sleep, self-esteem, and anxiety. The results, presented at the British Psychological Society's Developmental and Social Psychology Annual Conference, are exactly what we would expect them to be. Folks feel pressure from social media to be online and available all the time. This fear of missing some deep connection is also fostered by the fact that the majority of people only present the positive experiences of their life online (job advances, parties, vacations, etc.).

When we send an email, we expect a reply within a few days. When we send a text, we expect a reply within minutes. According to Dr. Woods, this pressure can cause a fear of "missing out" on personal connections or important news, resulting in anxiety, poor sleep, and even depression.

Most people realize that posts, tweets, and texts are not a substitute for interpersonal interactions. However, they do represent a connecting point with family and friends, and those people matter to us. The stress of staying connected increases if we are feeling disconnected from relationships in general. When we feel alone, it is easy to look to online friends for quick support. And sadly, it is easy to imagine that your lone electronic voice is not connecting with anyone.

Yoked to Jesus

If fear of missing out on a friend's comment leads us to an almost obsessive need to check our Facebook status, or if we are simply feeling uncomfortably distant from family and friends, we need to reconsider Paul's words.

"Do not be anxious about anything, but in every situation, by prayer and petition, with thanksgiving, present your requests to God. And the peace of God, which transcends all understanding, will guard your hearts and your minds in Christ Jesus." (Philippians 4:6-7)

Paul encourages us to draw near to God and share our anxieties and requests as well as words of praise. Prayer is not about sounding eloquent, but coming into the presence of God who desires to help us. His words echo the teaching of Jesus.

"Come to me, all you who are weary and burdened, and I will give you rest. Take my yoke upon you and learn from me, for I am gentle and humble in heart, and you will find rest for your souls. For my yoke is easy and my burden is light."
(Matthew 11:28-30)

The image of a yoke would have made sense to the agrarian culture of Jesus' day. It may make a little less sense to those of us who have not worked on a farm. A yoke is the wooden crosspiece that fastens over the necks of two animals and attaches to the plow or cart that they pull. The yoke enables the two to work together, so that neither is left with the full weight of their burden.

Jesus invites us to be yoked with him. This is an invitation for more than mere "connection." Christ wants to help with whatever load we carry. The word "easy" in this context means the yoke fits well. An easy yoke is the right shape and size for the person wearing it. The relationship which Christ offers is not intended to be another burden weighing us down. Jesus desires that we find rest by allowing him to come alongside us and help bear our burdens.

"So do not fear, for I am with you;
  do not be dismayed, for I am your God.
I will strengthen you and help you;
  I will uphold you with my righteous right hand."
(Isaiah 41:10)

A Spiritual Practice

As noted earlier, Paul encourages us to work toward a life of prayer. I find prayer to be one of the most rewarding of the spiritual practices - and the most difficult to discuss. That is because prayer takes on as many different forms as there are people and is often misunderstood.

Scripture writers assume prayer is an essential part of every believer's life. There are so many biblical passages which refer to prayer, or are prayers themselves, that it is difficult to count them. Prayer is any communication we offer to God, verbal or nonverbal, written or oral.

Too often people reduce prayer to our telling God what we want. In healthy prayer, we not only share our authentic self with our Creator, but we listen for what God is saying to us. We must train ourselves to listen to the Spirit from a variety of sources: an audible voice, scripture (as in "divine reading"), the words of others, intuitive awareness, opportunities that arise, etc. Meditation and contemplation are powerful forms of prayer since they involve listening by opening our heart and mind to God's presence.

While it is important to be honest in prayer and say what is on our minds, the goal of prayer is not to convince God of something. Rather, we should ask God to move us so we are in alignment with what God desires. We should always follow our prayer requests with something like "but in the end, I believe you know more about what I need than I do. Help me to surrender my desires for my life to what you desire to accomplish in me." (Matthew 26:36-39) Without this thought permeating our prayers, we are tempted to believe that if God is real or loving, then God will do what we desire. This makes God our servant instead of seeing ourselves as children of God.

There are dozens of methods and styles of prayer. Since everyone is unique, there is no one form of prayer that will automatically fit you. You must find your own path. But that is not to say there are not helpful suggestions to be made. For some, sitting in silence is the best way to experience the presence of God. For others, silence is incredibly distracting. They need to be walking or driving in order to pray. Your prayers might last a few minutes or an hour.

Likewise, some of us should be praying first thing in the morning; others of us need to pray mid-day; a few of us need to pray in the evening. What matters is that we offer God our best - for our sake! If we are half asleep in the morning and offer half-hearted prayers, then we will miss out on the connection for which we long. We may continue this sort of mediocre prayer life out of sheer will, but we won't come closer to discovering what it means to rest in peace of God's presence.

What matters most is finding a time, place, and method which fits your personality and temperament. Jesus' yoke is supposed to be easy.

"As Jesus and his disciples were on their way, he came to a village where a woman named Martha opened her home to him. She had a sister called Mary, who sat at the Lord's feet listening to what he said. But Martha was distracted by all the preparations that had to be made. She came to him and asked, 'Lord, don't you care that my sister has left me to do the work by myself? Tell her to help me!'

'Martha, Martha,' the Lord answered, 'you are worried and upset about many things, but few things are needed—or indeed only one. Mary has chosen what is better, and it will not be taken away from her'." (Luke 10:38-42)

 Mary found her place of rest; Martha had not. There is nothing wrong with working around the house. Some of us are able to focus on God when we are puttering about, but Martha is worried and upset. Isn't that amazing?! She is literally standing in the presence of Jesus, but she cannot focus on his presence or find peace.

We are in the presence of God, right now, wherever we are. The question is whether we will bring our anxieties to God through prayer and rest in that connection.

Here is a basic pattern for prayer. Adjust it to fit your life. 1) Determine a time and place that will allow you to offer God your full attention. Sit in silence for a few moments. Take a few deep breaths. Most of us need this preparation time to settle our thoughts and focus on being present.

2) Remember who God is and who you are. Whether aloud or silently to yourself, put your thoughts and feelings into words of praise to God your Creator. For many of us, this prayer of "adoration" will naturally lead to one of two paths: confession or thanksgiving. Both forms of prayer are important. Begin with one and then proceed to the other.

3) A prayer of confession acknowledges your sin and seeks to be reconciled to God. The more honest and detailed you can be - listing the ways you have failed and expressing your feelings - the more you will discover your need and desire for forgiveness.

4) A prayer of thanksgiving acknowledges the blessings in your life, thanking God for each.

5) Next, offer prayers for the needs of others and then, yourself. It is best to offer prayers of "supplication" for yourself last because recalling the state of others gives some perspective to our needs and desires.

6) After you have offered these various prayers, sit in silence, becoming aware of the presence of God and listening (becoming aware) for what God might be communicating to you.

Chapter Four - Be Part of Something Bigger

I grew up in a middle class suburb in Knoxville, Tennessee. I spent my free time as a child swimming at a community pool, playing on recreation sports teams, and running around our neighborhood with friends. From an early age, my parents felt comfortable letting me walk everywhere unsupervised. Well, unsupervised by them. The parents of whoever's house or yard we chose that day became the supervision for all the kids. Trust me when I say that if a neighborhood "mom" caught you doing something inappropriate, she would have no qualms about calling your parents with the news or just handing out punishment herself!

Something has happened over the last thirty or forty years. Blame whoever you like, but neighborhoods are not the same anymore. My family has lived in three houses over the last ten years. In the first two locations, we were, at best, acquaintances with those living around us. One of the joys of our current home is that we have a handful of wonderful neighbors with whom we socialize. However, even now we do not know everyone on our street. Heck, I don't even know the name of the guy who lives cattycorner from us. We count ourselves blessed to have friends in four homes around us with whom we enjoy spending time.

Perhaps the allure of television keeps us indoors. Maybe the increase of two career families contributes. At times I think the proliferation of lawsuits has made everyone a little afraid. We know that correcting a naughty child in a grocery store might mean a confrontation with parents who do not want our "help." It seems people no longer trust one another. I do not have any statistical data to prove my theories on neighborliness, but plenty of anecdotal evidence exists to suggest that we feel a growing sense of isolation from one another.

The National Science Foundation recently reported that an increasing number of Americans are lonely. Sociologists at Duke and the University of Arizona surveyed 1,500 people in face-to-face interviews and discovered more than 25% of those studied said they have nobody with whom to talk about personal struggles or victories. If family members were excluded from the results, the number of lonely individuals doubles to more than 50%! Their research found an increase in general "social isolation" and a significant decrease in the connections people have with friends and family.

These findings have been confirmed in other studies as well. The 2006 American Sociological Review found that 25% of Americans living in 2004 had no confidants in their lives. In 1985, that number had been 10%. After examination of Census Bureau data, the Beverly LaHaye Institute reported that from 1960 to 2000, the percentage of people not living in a family group nearly tripled, from 6 to 16%. About 70% of those persons lived alone.

We are losing our sense of community. This is more than a commentary about feeling sad or alone. Living in increasing isolation from one another contributes to our general state of anxiety.

Becoming a Community of Peace

As we noted in the last chapter, scripture assumes that we were created for relationship with God and one another. Of course, biblical writers emphasize that our connection with God must be a priority. When we think about it, this makes sense. As wonderful as friends and family are, if we demand that spouse, children, or anyone else provide purpose and direction for our lives, a role only God can fulfill, we put our loved ones in a no-win situation. They cannot satisfy our deepest yearnings anymore that we can provide ultimate meaning for someone else.

But it should also be noted that our greatest ally for finding and maintaining a healthy relationship with God is a community of faithful friends. Here is one of many passages found in scripture, where the writer assumes that the peace of God is found in the loving unity we have with one another.

"Therefore, as God's chosen people, holy and dearly loved, clothe yourselves with compassion, kindness, humility, gentleness and patience. Bear with each other and forgive one another if any of you has a grievance against someone. Forgive as the Lord forgave you. And over all these virtues put on love, which binds them all together in perfect unity.

Let the peace of Christ rule in your hearts, since as members of one body you were called to peace. And be thankful. Let the message of Christ dwell among you richly as you teach and admonish one another with all wisdom through psalms, hymns, and songs from the Spirit, singing to God with gratitude in your hearts. And whatever you do, whether in word or deed, do it all in the name of the Lord Jesus, giving thanks to God the Father through him." (Colossians 3:12-17)

In the biblical tradition, "peace of Christ" implies more than simply an absence of war or a passing feeling of relaxation. It refers to the fullness of joy and life that is found when we are in a good and healthy relationship with God. The "peace of Christ" becomes the foundation on which we build real community. I can offer compassion, kindness, etc. to others because I have experienced those gifts myself in my connection with Christ. The more a people draw near to God, the more their community should reflect the love and compassion of Jesus.

Unfortunately, we are all too aware that Christians do not always embody such Christ-like attitudes toward each   other or those outside the church. Followers of Jesus have hurt many people. That is sad and tragic, especially when we realize God's desire is for us to be THE place of love and acceptance. The people of God should be the ones who are working to be real community for each other.

If you have been hurt by those who consider themselves Christian, I am sorry. Please realize you are not alone. All of us have been wounded at one time or another by those who actions are not in line with Jesus.

However, we need to acknowledge that not everyone who shows up on a Sunday morning for worship is mature, loving, or kind. We let anyone and everyone come to Church, not just the loving and righteous people! If we tried to stop everyone at the door who has issues, nobody would be welcome to worship. And I guarantee none of our pastors would make that cut!

When we encounter people who are mean-spirited or cold, we should not assume they represent God or the entire Church. How would you like it if everyone thought you must be hard hearted and cruel because they met someone from your work or school who is mean and callous? I am not trying to excuse the intolerant and spiteful behavior of people calling themselves Christians. Just the opposite. I think we should heed the advice of scripture and try to help everyone understand what it means to *"clothe yourselves with compassion, kindness, humility, gentleness and patience."* It really matters that we act like a community! We have to choose to bear with one another's weaknesses and forgive one another's failures.

Of course, there is a flip side to saying "we let everyone in, warts and all." The Church should never, never pretend to be "holier than thou." Nothing is more annoying that Christians whose words and actions proclaim, "we are perfect - when you have your act together, then you can join us!" God keep us from that tragedy! As my grandmother might have said, "God bless their hearts." Followers of Jesus should be the ones most aware of their issues and failures. And that is why all people are welcome!

Jesus knows his disciples are not perfect. He loves them anyway. He is accused of hanging around with people who the religious establishment avoided! One of his twelve closest disciples is a tax collector. In first century Palestine, tax collectors work for the Roman Empire, the dreaded foreign oppressors who occupy the land through military force.

"As Jesus went on from there, he saw a man named Matthew sitting at the tax collector's booth. 'Follow me,' he told him, and Matthew got up and followed him. While Jesus was having dinner at Matthew's house, many tax collectors and sinners came and ate with him and his disciples. When the Pharisees saw this, they asked his disciples, 'Why does your teacher eat with tax collectors and sinners?' On hearing this, Jesus said, 'It is not the healthy who need a doctor, but the sick. But go and learn what this means: "I desire mercy, not sacrifice." For I have not come to call the righteous, but sinners." (Matthew 9:9-13)

Jesus understands that we all need God's forgiveness and grace. Some of us realize that; some of us don't. And Jesus knows that it is not going to be easy for his followers to act like a real community. Immediately before his arrest and crucifixion, he prays for his disciples and those who will believe because of their words.

"My prayer is not for them alone. I pray also for those who will believe in me through their message, that all of them may be one, Father, just as you are in me and I am in you. May they also be in us so that the world may believe that you have sent me. I have given them the glory that you gave me, that they may be one as we are one— I in them and you in me—so that they may be brought to complete unity. Then the world will know that you sent me and have loved them even as you have loved me." (John 17:20-23)

Fascinating, isn't it? We are to show grace and compassion to one another because we first experience them in the presence of God. Grace and compassion becomes the foundation for our unity in the community of faith. That unity becomes a sign of God's love for the world which draws more people to experience the presence of God.

It matters that we belong to a community that not only works toward internal unity but also welcomes all people, treating them with respect and compassion. We do not have to agree on everything (biblically, theologically, politically, socially, ethically, etc.) to demonstrate "compassion, kindness, humility, gentleness and patience." When shared with one another, those gifts become an entry point for encountering the peace of Christ.

A Spiritual Practice

The first time I read a book on spiritual practices, I was not surprised that prayer, scripture reading, and meditation were discussed. I was shocked and pleasantly surprised to discover that not all the topics were as "ethereal" as those. I had no idea that followers of Jesus had forever associated service to others as a potential "spiritual" encounter.

I knew my time working on Habitat for Humanity homes felt deeply rewarding. Growing up I had always enjoyed helping Mr. James, the elderly bachelor that lived across the street. It made me feel great to do odd jobs for him or mow the lawn. As I read about how service offered with grace toward others can draw us closer to God, I knew that this was a spiritual practice that made sense to me. I am not alone. For many, serving others is the most rewarding aspect of their spiritual life.

"Each of you should use whatever gift you have received to serve others, as faithful stewards of God's grace in its various forms. If anyone speaks, they should do so as one who speaks the very words of God. If anyone serves, they should do so with the strength God provides, so that in all things God may be praised through Jesus Christ. To him be the glory and the power for ever and ever. Amen." (1 Peter 4:10-11)

Peter reminds us that our intentions have a great deal to do with whether an act of service makes us more aware of God's presence. There are many reasons to serve others. Peter simply wants us to be mindful. Do you want to experience the presence of God? Then respond to God's grace for you by finding a way to show a little grace to others.

However, we don't have to be so heavenly minded that we pray every other moment or quote scripture to the people we are serving. When I mowed Mr. James' yard, I was not thinking about responding to God's grace; I just wanted to help him out. And sometimes that is enough. The questions are "what is our desire? Where is our heart?" Many of us have started out to show a little kindness to someone only to discover God's presence right there in the moment.

By the way, one way to test where your heart is while performing an act of service is to ask if you expect or demand a response from the person you are serving. Service as a spiritual practice is driven by a desire to respond to God's call to serve others and perform good works whether the world or anyone in particular acknowledges it or not. Our focus should remain on our connection to God as much as possible. In serving others, we remember how God cares for us. It is wonderful when people show appreciation for our service, but if you find yourself being upset because people are not appreciative enough, then you have probably moved from an act of spiritual practice to trying to earn something.

There is nothing wrong with serving for other reasons, but you will want to step back, take a deep breathe, and reassess the situation. We can learn a lot about ourselves in those moments. Just as nobody can pray all the time, it might be that you are simply tired and need to rest.

In fact, sitting quietly and reflecting on a gift of service you have offered is a wonderful way to bring this spiritual practice to a conclusion.

Be aware of the presence of God and discover the peace that comes in knowing that you are a part of something bigger than yourself. When we serve others in the name of Christ, we are part of a community striving to demonstrate to others the care and kindness that God has shown to us.

That is the way to discover peace in our own lives.

"Let us therefore make every effort to do what leads to peace and to mutual edification." (Romans 14:19)

Chapter Five - Take a Deep Breath

When I came into work this morning, I did what I always do: made coffee, glanced at my calendar, checked email… and promptly became distracted by some website links friends had sent me. One of those was a link inviting people to slowing inhale and exhale. It provided a graphic of a small circle expanding and contracting, reminiscent of lungs, to help people remember to breathe. You can find a copy of it at christchurchchatt.org/dev/images/stories/book/RSoEELO.gif.

Of course, I was breathing already, but not those slow, full breaths that fill my body with rest. The sad reality is that we can go for days without breathing deeply. So many of us share this common experience that "take a deep breath" has become a catchphrase for "slow down, pause for a moment, and reflect on the situation." Believe it or not, that is good advice on both a physical and spiritual level.

The word "breath" is a really interesting word biblically. Both the Hebrew "ruach" and Greek "pneuma" can be translated breath, wind, or spirit. This helps explain some very interesting passages of scripture. For instance, Genesis 2:7 says the Lord God formed the first human *"from the dust of the ground and breathed into his nostrils the breath of life."*

This refers to more than expanding lungs with air. God gives life to our spirit.

When we talk about a person's spirit, we refer to the nonphysical side of who they are. If we compare someone's appearance at 100 years old to a photo taken at their birth, they look physically quite different. Science tells us that every cell in their body has changed or been replaced. If that is the case, what makes them the same person? What makes you "you?"

Scripture says you are more than your physical body. Your body will change, but you are the same person. The essence of who we are remains the same.

The writer of Genesis reminds us that our spirit, enlivened by the breath of God, is a gift. Our life, experienced one breath at a time, is a gift.

We do not have to understand Hebrew or Greek to experience the power of slowing down to take a deep breath. Almost every religious tradition has a spiritual practice of thoughtfully concentrating on breathing as a way to refocus on what matters and savor the gift of life.

Following his resurrection, when Jesus wanted to communicate the living presence of God to his followers, he drew on this same biblical connection between spirit and breath.

"On the evening of that first day of the week, when the disciples were together, with the doors locked for fear of the Jewish leaders, Jesus came and stood among them and said, 'Peace be with you!' After he said this, he showed them his hands and side. The disciples were overjoyed when they saw the Lord. Again Jesus said, 'Peace be with you! As the Father has sent me, I am sending you.' And with that he breathed on them and said, 'Receive the Holy Spirit'." (John 20:19-29)

Just as the Creator breathes life into our spirit, Christ offers the gift of the Holy Spirit to guide and encourage us. We should notice that when Jesus talks about the gift of God's Spirit, he links it to finding peace.

Feeling Helpless

I am a pretty calm person. When I am angry or stressed, I can usually remain level-headed and control my emotions. But I lose all composure when I see someone being bullied. It doesn't matter if the bully is using emotional, verbal, or physical coercion to intimidate, I lose all compassion for that person. God only knows what I might say to that "child of God." I am not suggesting this is a good or Christ-like response. Following the example of Jesus, it would be better if I intervened in a way that shows kindness to everyone involved as well as seeks justice. But I have a long way to go to be that person.

The reason I respond as I do probably goes back to being a rather small child and a younger brother. I don't remember being bullied as a child, but it was always one of my fears growing up. I hate the feeling of being helpless. All those childhood fears rush back when I see someone placed in a situation where they appear helpless.

One of the most common descriptions of anxiety is "feeling helpless and hopeless." We will cover the Bible's response to "hopeless" soon enough, but for now, we can celebrate that it has a lot to say about feeling helpless.

Jesus promises to give the gift of the Holy Spirit to his followers long before he breathes its presence on them. Prior to his arrest, Jesus gathers the twelve together, shares the Passover meal with them, and washes their feet. He knows their life is about to take a terrible, unexpected turn. They do not understand what is about to happen. They are still waiting on him to rise up and use his miraculous powers to extinguish his enemies. Knowing they will feel helpless in just a few hours, he comforts them. You can hear their confusion, even as Jesus sets them on a path toward peace.

"Do not let your hearts be troubled. You believe in God; believe also in me. My Father's house has many rooms; if that were not so, would I have told you that I am going there to prepare a

place for you? And if I go and prepare a place for you, I will come back and take you to be with me that you also may be where I am. You know the way to the place where I am going."

"Thomas said to him, 'Lord, we don't know where you are going, so how can we know the way?'

"Jesus answered, 'I am the way and the truth and the life. No one comes to the Father except through me. If you really know me, you will know my Father as well. From now on, you do know him and have seen him.'

"Philip said, 'Lord, show us the Father and that will be enough for us.'

"Jesus answered: 'Don't you know me, Philip, even after I have been among you such a long time? Anyone who has seen me has seen the Father. How can you say, "Show us the Father"?'

"If you love me, keep my commands. And I will ask the Father, and he will give you another advocate to help you and be with you forever— the Spirit of truth. The world cannot accept

him, because it neither sees him nor knows him. But you know
him, for he lives with you and will be in you. I will not leave you
as orphans; I will come to you. Before long, the world will not
see me anymore, but you will see me. Because I live, you also will
live.

"All this I have spoken while still with you. But the Advocate , the
Holy Spirit, whom the Father will send in my name, will teach
you all things and will remind you of everything I have said to
you. Peace I leave with you; my peace I give you. I do not give to
you as the world gives. Do not let your hearts be troubled and
do not be afraid."
(John 14:1-9, 15-19, 25-27)

They are not able to hear his promise of help in that moment, but we can. His description of the Spirit, the presence of God, gives us insight into how to find peace when we feel anxious.

The Holy Spirit is described as the Advocate. The Greek word being translated is "parakletos." It is a complex term which other scholars translate as "Comforter," "Counselor," and

"Helper." Each of these choices have subtle connotations, but the point is clear: God is present and on our side.

Do you ever feel helpless, alone, overwhelmed by forces too great for you? Jesus says the presence of God is available for those who open themselves to it. There is no magic incantation that awakens the Spirit. You don't have to be perfect for God to show up. When we turn toward God in humility, commit ourselves to following the way Jesus teaches, and decide to follow wherever God leads, we experience the presence of the Spirit. And our Advocate brings peace.

"Peace I leave with you; my peace I give you. I do not give to you as the world gives. Do not let your hearts be troubled and do not be afraid." (John 14:27)

Jesus knows we have heard the promise of "peace" thrown around by politicians and hucksters. We have been sold all kind of gadgets and quick techniques that promise peace. That is why he clarifies - his peace is not like that offered by the world. The presence of God brings comfort and counsel. The Holy Spirit desires to help us right where we are. These wonderful words are all the more powerful when we remember that Jesus spoke them knowing that he was soon to be arrested, convinced, and crucified. To be led by the Spirit is to discover the peace of Christ no matter the outward circumstances.

A New Normal

However, we should note that it is no small matter to say "turn toward God in humility." There is a reason Jesus uses the phrase "Spirit of truth" alongside the "Advocate." In Chapter Two we discussed the importance of being honest with God about everything: sins, blessings, fears, gifts, abilities, and doubts. We do not want to make the mistake of thinking that asking for the Spirit's help to find peace means that once our anxiety passes everything returns to what has been up to that point "normal."

Opening ourselves to the Advocate means there is a new "normal!" The Spirit of truth calls us to deeper levels of peace which are found when we avoid committing the same sins, acknowledge our blessings, face our fears, use our gifts, enhance our abilities, and act faithfully in spite of our doubts. Some of these are very difficult! Taking some of these steps of faith requires our best efforts. But do not be afraid. We are not alone on this journey. That is the point! God will be with us. We do not have to see the entire path to take the one step we do see in front of us.

"I have much more to say to you, more than you can now bear. But when he, the Spirit of truth, comes, he will guide you into all the truth." (John 16:12-13)

Jesus knew his disciples were not capable of hearing about all that lie ahead. None of us are. It takes all we have to deal with the issues that are immediately before us. So the promise of God is not just that the Spirit is with us, but that the Spirit of truth will continue to call and guide us forward.

A Spiritual Practice

Take a deep breath.

One of the more ancient methods of becoming aware of the presence of God is called "breath prayer." This practice uses a short prayer phrase that captures a deep yearning we have for God. This prayer uses the rhythm of our breath, inhaling as we pray a short phrase and then exhaling as we pray a short phrase. The increased awareness of our breathing is a reminder of our physical and spiritual dependence on God. Not surprisingly, there are many variations on this practice, and you should adapt it for yourself.

The best-known breath prayer is called the Jesus Prayer: "Lord Jesus Christ, Son of God, have mercy on me." To offer this prayer, you slowly inhale and pray, "Lord Jesus Christ." Pause between inhaling and exhaling to pray, "Son of God." As you exhale, pray, "have mercy on me."

A more complex form of breathe prayer invites you to create the words you will pray as you breathe. Begin by asking God to help you form a breath prayer. Take your time and think about your favorite name for God. For some it might be "God," while others might use Jesus, Holy Spirit, Wisdom, Creator God, Source of Life, or Higher Power. Choose the name or image that resonates deeply with you.

Next, reflect for a moment on what it is you need or want to express in your prayer. Choose a short phrase that speaks to you and can be spoken in one breath.

Place these two parts together in any way you like.

Jesus Christ, send your peace

God, forgive me

Lord, hear my prayer

Guide me, Holy Spirit

Heal me, Loving God

Once you determine what your breath prayer will be, use it by inhaling on the first part and exhaling on the second part.

 Repeat the prayer, silently or aloud. Before long, you will find that you are "breathing the prayer." Allow the breath prayer to gently lead you to a place of inner peace and calm. At some point, you might discover that you don't need to say the words any more. If that happens, stay in that moment of contemplation, allowing God's presence to comfort you.

The Spirit of God has made me;
the breath of the Almighty gives me life.
(Job 33:4)

Chapter Six - Learn to Lament and Celebrate

Our family loves to watch movies together. One of the joys of modern life is that we have so many options from which to choose each night sitting in our living room. Of course, the difficulty is finding a movie on which we will all agree.

Annette and I have a fairly easy time; we both enjoy action-adventure comedies. However, she will be the first to tell you that what she really likes are sentimental Lifetime movies where the two people in love end up together. When our younger daughter gets added to the mix, picking a movie that excites the three of us is more difficult. She prefers documentaries, off-beat comedies, and zombie flicks. If we include our daughter and son-in-law...well it takes a rare alignment of the stars to make any movie acceptable to all of us.

One problem we face in selecting a movie everyone enjoys is that our older daughter does not like to watch movies she deems "sad." By this, she does not mean films that have a depressing ending. She avoids all movies which have a sad moment in them. Well, even characters in comedies face difficulties that are "sad." Filmmakers do this on purpose and not because they are a depressed group of people. They understand the power of catharsis.

Catharsis is that feeling of relief we feel when we see someone overcome difficult odds. It is the cleansing and contentment we experience when built up emotions such as pity and fear are released, becoming joy and triumph. Artists understand the power catharsis has on us, so they tailor their films, songs, and plays to enable us to ride that emotional wave. Endings are "happy" because someone has been victorious in the face of defeat, discovered love, or found a way to make sure good wins and evil does not.

Our daughter enjoys that cathartic feeling as much as anyone. If she does not know the plot of a movie, she gets caught up in the story and experiences the relief of a happy ending as much as the rest of us. It is the anticipation of the sadness that she does not like. And I must admit I understand that. She and I are cut from the same cloth in many ways. I do not like "sad" moments in films either. As Annette points out, she watches

Lifetime movies because she knows that everything will work out and be happy.

Unfortunately, this minor inconvenience our family experiences in selecting entertainment is actually reflective of a larger cultural issue. Too many of us refuse to accept any negative feelings as a normal part of life.

Emotional Avoidance

According to recent research, one cause of many modern psychological struggles is the habit of emotional avoidance. Obviously nobody likes to feel bad, and there are times when ignoring a temporary negative feeling is perfectly reasonable. If someone cuts you off in traffic, it is healthy to let go of that initial rush of anger rather than dwelling on it. However, some people try to avoid negative feelings at all costs. That is when it becomes a problem.

Life is not easy, but overcoming obstacles is how we grow emotionally strong and build important skills. It takes thousands of hours of effort for a toddler to develop the basic skills of life: walking, talking, dexterity, etc. How many times does an average child fall down while learning to walk? How many Cheerios are dropped on the way to the mouth? How many tears are shed learning to share or go to sleep? Thank goodness children do not fear those obstacles so much that they just give up!

It might seem that avoiding negative emotions would be the path to an easier, happier life. But ironically, the opposite is true. The more we avoid the difficulties and negatives of life, the weaker we become, the more our coping mechanisms diminish, and the less abundance we experience in life. In fact, trying to avoid negative feelings simply creates more and more fear of possible disappointments that might result from every path from which we must choose. Is there ever a way forward in life that doesn't result in at least the possibility of unpleasantness?

Most of us realize the anxiety that results from worrying about something which might take place is quite often worse than the actual experience when it occurs. That is because our anxiety is not limited by reality. When we try hard not to worry, our minds rush to the worst case scenarios. A mind driven by anxiety finds that the gift of imagination can become a nightmare.

Perhaps this is a result of our culture's steady diet of thirty minute sitcoms. After all, there is no problem so horrible that a television family cannot solve it in a single episode. Finding an entertaining movie that provides a respite from "reality" is one thing, but we need to remember no one has a life devoid of issues.

It seems to me emotional avoidance is probably a quite common secondary cause of anxiety for many of us. If we are already struggling with a state of generalized anxiety, we probably have a tendency to think "I cannot tolerate one more negative thing."

Learning to Cry Out

Low tolerance for emotional pain is one of the causes of anxiety I see most obviously demonstrated on a communal level in churches. Everybody loves "happy" holy days such as

Christmas (remembering Jesus' birth) and Easter (his resurrection), so attendance at those celebrations is usually quite high. However, days such as Holy Thursday (Jesus shares the Lord's Supper, washes the disciple's feet, and is arrested) and Good Friday (his crucifixion and death) have very low attendance, even among dedicated Christians.

But those holy days which "celebrate" the difficult aspects of Jesus' story are essential if we want to understand and appreciate the love of God or the joy of resurrection!

I believe another example of collective emotional avoidance occurs on Palm Sunday, the day we celebrate Jesus' arrival in Jerusalem prior to his crucifixion on Friday. There are two very distinct emotional aspects to the events of that day. On the one hand, the crowd celebrates the arrival of Jesus with parade-like joy, welcoming Jesus and shouting praise. On the other hand, this is the same crowd that will abandon him in a few days, calling for his crucifixion. And in just a few years in the future, the entire city will be destroyed by the Roman legions. So, the crowd's excitement that a new King has come to save the nation is doubly sad for him, knowing the pain that lies ahead for them.

Jesus grasps both sides of this emotional situation. He receives their words of praise and honors their joy, but he also gives himself over to the sadness of the moment.

"After Jesus had said this, he went on ahead, going up to Jerusalem. As he approached Bethphage and Bethany at the hill called the Mount of Olives, he sent two of his disciples, saying to them, 'Go to the village ahead of you, and as you enter it, you will find a colt tied there, which no one has ever ridden. Untie it and bring it here. If anyone asks you, "Why are you untying it?" say, "The Lord needs it".'

"Those who were sent ahead went and found it just as he had told them. As they were untying the colt, its owners asked them, 'Why are you untying the colt?'

"They replied, 'The Lord needs it.'

"They brought it to Jesus, threw their cloaks on the colt and put Jesus on it. As he went along, people spread their cloaks on the

road.

"When he came near the place where the road goes down the Mount of Olives, the whole crowd of disciples began joyfully to praise God in loud voices for all the miracles they had seen: 'Blessed is the king who comes in the name of the Lord!' 'Peace in heaven and glory in the highest!'

"Some of the Pharisees in the crowd said to Jesus, 'Teacher, rebuke your disciples!'

"'I tell you,' he replied, 'if they keep quiet, the stones will cry out.'

"As he approached Jerusalem and saw the city, he wept over it and said, 'If you, even you, had only known on this day what would bring you peace—but now it is hidden from your eyes. The days will come upon you when your enemies will build an embankment against you and encircle you and hem you in on every side. They will dash you to the ground, you and the children within your walls. They will not leave one stone on another, because you did not recognize the time of God's coming to you.'" (Luke 19:28-44)

Jesus is honest. He does not ignore the painful aspects of life but embraces them. Throughout the week leading up to his crucifixion, he teaches about the failures of the religious leaders as well as pointing out the faith of the poor widow (Luke 20:45-21:4). He shares a meal with this beloved disciples, but does not hesitate to point out their upcoming betrayal (Luke 22:7-34). He acknowledges God's presence even as he laments the path toward the cross he must walk (Luke 22:39-46).

At the resurrection, God does not go back in time and do away with the pain of Jesus' journey. God redeems the pain, brining victory out of those dark moments. And that is key.

The purpose of lament is not to wallow in negative emotions or merely grumble with anger. Lament is about giving voice to our doubts, fears, and desires because we believe God has promised to never leave us. Pain propels us forward to search with all of who we are, holding nothing back. That search invites us to look at ourselves honestly, to abandon apathy, and to surrender ourselves to the hope that if God can bring resurrection from a cross, then God can bring light to our darkness. To lament is to express faith that God is still with us, still listening, still cares.

For centuries the followers of Jesus assumed celebration and lament were equally important aspects of a healthy spiritual life. Like our Jewish ancestors, the early church sang psalms of lament as a way of confessing not only the difficulties in the world, but their own confusion about how to move forward into the future. Passages such as Psalm 80, Jeremiah's Lamentation, and Jesus' prayers in the Garden of Gethsemane (Matthew 26:36-46) provided the backdrop for their own crying out to God.

"How long, LORD? Will you forget me forever?
   How long will you hide your face from me?
How long must I wrestle with my thoughts
   and day after day have sorrow in my heart?
   How long will my enemy triumph over me?

"Look on me and answer, LORD my God.
   Give light to my eyes, or I will sleep in death,
and my enemy will say, "I have overcome him,"

and my foes will rejoice when I fall.

"But I trust in your unfailing love;
  my heart rejoices in your salvation.
I will sing the LORD's praise,
  for he has been good to me. (Psalm 13)

An amazing thing happens when we read or sing songs of lament together: we are reminded that we are not alone. Pain tends to separate us. But when we tell our stories of loss and fear, we rediscover that others have felt or are currently feeling the same sorrow.

There is great power in listening to each other. There is no compassion so powerful as that which is offered by someone who has walked the same lonely path. As much as I may have disliked the hardest periods in my life, they absolutely have made me have deep empathy for those who currently suffer those same circumstances. When a woman in our church receives a diagnosis of breast cancer, who are the first people to run to her side? That is right: breast cancer survivors who know how isolated and frightened she is.

Having someone express love by listening and connecting with someone who understands is life-changing. We can hear Paul struggle with just such a concept in his letter to the followers of Jesus in Rome.

"Therefore, since we have been justified through faith, we have peace with God through our Lord Jesus Christ, through whom we have gained access by faith into this grace in which we now stand. And we boast in the hope of the glory of God. Not only so, but we also glory in our sufferings, because we know that suffering produces perseverance; perseverance, character; and character, hope. And hope does not put us to shame, because God's love has been poured out into our hearts through the Holy Spirit, who has been given to us." (Romans 5:1-5)

Lament is never supposed to be an end in itself. It opens our heart to wrestle with a God who understands what it means to suffer and desires for us to rest in the promise of the Holy Spirit's presence and our future with God.

We are not alone. The negative emotions we experience do not have to overwhelm us. They may be unpleasant for a time, but we do not have to fear them so much that we become anxious about avoiding them. Which brings us to the important distinction between happiness and joy.

Happiness and Joy

The Bible does not say a great deal about happiness. That is because being happiness is an emotional state. It is a great thing to feel positive, but emotions come and go. We do not choose how we feel. But joy - that is a different matter. The Bible tells people all the time to "rejoice," to be joyful! That is because joy is not an emotion but a way to look at life.

Joy is an orientation toward celebration and delight in the good gifts of creation which arises from an awareness of God's presence and promises. Joy is a deep sense of contentment based on the awareness that God is ultimately on our side. Joy sees the good in the moment even if the only good is that God is with us and will not abandon us. Joy knows that our current trials do not diminish our future with God.

My happiness may fluctuate depending on whether my team is winning or what I am having for dinner. My joy is built on

God's unfailing love. That is why there is a direct correlation between our awareness of God's presence and the extent of our joy (Galatians 5:22).

That is why Jesus is able to look at the good and bad of each moment without becoming anxious. He models for us how to be completely open and vulnerable in prayer (Luke 22: 39-46) and then to move forward with calm determination toward the cross . He believes there is a resurrection on the other side of pain (Luke 18:31-33). The joy of that coming day sustains him through his most difficult times.

The joy of our future with God can sustain us as well. We can embrace all of life, allowing the more negative feelings to move us toward strength, maturity, and compassion for others. We can learn to sing songs of lament as well as celebration, trusting in God in both circumstances.

"Do not fret because of the those who are evil
or be envious of those who do wrong;
for like the grass they will soon wither,
like green plants they will soon die away.

Trust in the Lord and do good;

    dwell in the land and enjoy safe pasture.

Take delight in the Lord,

    and he will give you the desires of your heart.

Commit your way to the Lord;

    trust in him ad he will do this:

He will make your righteous reward shine like the dawn ,

    your vindication like the noonday sun.

Be still before the Lord

    and wait patiently for him;

do not fret when people succeed in their ways,

    when they carry out their wicked schemes."

(Psalm 37:1-7)

A Spiritual Practice

Certainly learning to include our laments and sorrows in our daily prayers is a valuable practice. However, there is another ancient form of spirituality that lends itself to finding peace in difficult emotional times: the Daily Examen.

This technique of prayerful reflection was first developed by Ignatius of Loyola, who believed God is always present and at work. The spiritual challenge according to him is to recognize how God is working and respond in gratitude and openness. The Examen invites us to reflect on the events of the day in order to detect God's presence and discern his direction for us.

Here is a brief description of the five-step Examen that St. Ignatius practiced:

1. Become aware of God's presence. This may take a few seconds or a few minutes.
2. Review the day with gratitude.
3. Pay attention to your emotions.
4. Choose one aspect of the day and allow it to form the foundation for your daily prayer.
5. Look toward tomorrow.

Most people find it useful to perform this review at the end of the day. The whole point of this self-examination is to become more God centered by observing how we acted and reacted throughout the day, especially noting how we interacted with God's Spirit. After we become comfortable with the practice, we begin to notice the subtle and unnoticed movements of God's Spirit in our lives. We see patterns that lead us to understand what brings energy and what drains our energy. Gratitude and confession are a natural part of this practice.

If you want more help with the "review" portion of the prayer, consider including one or more of the following questions in your reflection at the end of the day:

For what moment today am I most grateful?
For what moment today am I least grateful?
What was today's high point?
What was today's low point?
What was it today that was most life giving?
What was it today that was most life draining?
When today did I have the greatest sense of belonging to myself, others, and God?
When did I have the least sense of belonging today?

When did I sense connection with God?

When did I sense a disconnect with God?

When did I give and receive the most love today?

When did I give and receive the least love today?

When was I happiest today?

When was I saddest?

As you pray and reflect, remember that the goal is not to beat yourself up or ignore your struggles. Remember God is with you and desires for you to find peace, grow into the likeness of Christ, and become more aware of the Holy Spirit. You are a beloved child of God. You are not alone.

Chapter Seven- Find Light in the Darkness

I am 52 years old. I know something about having a mid-life crisis.

Like everything else related to the psychological and emotional states of human beings, there is no agreement on an exact definition of a midlife crisis. As Supreme Court Justice Potter Stewart said when asked how he could determine if a film was obscene or pornographic, "I know it when I see it." Most of us "mid-life" folk know the funk of crisis when we feel it.

A study of over two million people in eighty countries conducted by researchers at the University of Warwick and Dartmouth College found that people around the world experience a time of anxiety and depression during the period between youth and the senior years. Signs of midlife depression and anxiety strike people of all backgrounds and economic classes. In the United States, this mid-life anxiety often hits people in their 40s and 50s.

Obviously a mid-life crisis can be triggered by a variety of events. However most of the time it has to do with realizing the inevitability of death. People will point to other causes, such as being unhappy at work, having relationship issues, experiencing the maturation of children, grieving the death of a parent, and suffering the physical decline that comes with aging, but each of these are simply different ways of expressing the same issue of mortality. They are reminders that our time is limited and some of the dreams of our youth are not going to be fulfilled. We had hoped to achieve more or to find more happiness in the goals we have obtained. We begin to realize that we cannot start over. The trigger for our particular thought process may vary, but many of us look up one day to find ourselves facing the reality of death. When our mortality moves from the background of our thoughts to stand center stage, we frequently experience a feeling of hopelessness.

Feeling Hopeless

Sadly, people of all ages can feel hopeless. Not only can we feel the emotional weight of death at any age, we encounter other circumstances that can leave us feeling without hope. In their book "Hope in the Age of Anxiety," psychology professors Anthony Scioli and Henry Biller identify three distinctive types hopelessness common in our culture: 1) alienation – feeling forsaken and uninspired; 2) powerlessness – feeling oppressed and limited; 3) doom – feeling captive and helpless. These difficult emotions arise when one or more of our basic needs are compromised. Scioli and Biller define those essential needs as attachment, mastery, and survival. In short, we become anxious when we feel alone, incapable of positive action, or our life is threatened.

I find it encouraging to remember how easy it would have been for Jesus to feel this way. Surely he knows as well as anyone what it feels like to be abandoned, physically oppressed by others, and aware that his death is imminent. And yet, Jesus remains faithful and filled with hope in those most trying of days. That is why the events surrounding those days prior to his crucifixion are considered so important and holy for his followers. *"For we do not have a high priest (Jesus) who is unable to empathize with our weaknesses, but we have one who has been tempted in every way, just as we are—yet he did not sin."* (Hebrews 4:15) It is comforting to know that God has experienced physical and emotional pain. God understands.

Like us, Jesus knows he will die. Unlike most of us, he sees crucifixion at the hands of the religious leaders and government authorities clearly moving toward him. As he travels toward his arrest and execution in Jerusalem, Jesus foretells his death three times (Luke 9:21-27; 9:44-45; 18:31-34). But each time he acknowledges his upcoming death, he announces the good news of his future resurrection. *"And he said, 'The Son of Man must suffer many things and be rejected by the elders, the chief priests and the teachers of the law, and he must be killed and on the third day be raised to life'."* (Luke 9:21-22) Jesus faces the circumstances of hopelessness, but his faith in resurrection from the dead gives him hope.

He wants his disciples to know there is always hope when we are connected to the One who gives life. And Jesus is the high priest who connects us with God and eternal life.

"On his arrival, Jesus found that Lazarus had already been in the tomb for four days. Now Bethany was less than two miles from

Jerusalem, and many Jews had come to Martha and Mary to comfort them in the loss of their brother. When Martha heard that Jesus was coming, she went out to meet him, but Mary stayed at home.

'Lord,' Martha said to Jesus, 'if you had been here, my brother would not have died. But I know that even now God will give you whatever you ask.'

Jesus said to her, 'Your brother will rise again.'

Martha answered, 'I know he will rise again in the resurrection at the last day.'

Jesus said to her, 'I am the resurrection and the life. The one who believes in me will live, even though they die; and whoever lives by believing in me will never die. Do you believe this?'

'Yes, Lord,' she replied, 'I believe that you are the Messiah, the Son of God, who is to come into the world'." (John 11:17-27)

The good news is that God is with us, both in this life and beyond. God the Creator gives us birth into the world, provides new life through the Holy Spirit for those who will receive it, and promises those who seek him will discover a redeemed, resurrection life on the other side of our physical death.

The Easter Proclamation

The first funeral I ever attended was the first one I conducted after leaving seminary. When I was young, my parents went to funeral homes during "calling hours" when grieving families received friends, but my brother and I stayed home. Mom and Dad did not think funeral homes were appropriate places for children. By the time I was a teenager, I had no interest in attending what I was convinced must be dark and depressing ritual. I had grown up in a church hearing about Jesus' resurrection, but there seemed to be a divide between the theological teaching and the reality of death. I was convinced death was depressing and to be avoided.

We live in a culture that tries not to think about death. Theatrical deaths are acceptable because we know those actors are going to stand up and take a bow. Deaths in movies or video games do not bother us much because those are for entertainment - a disturbing thought that we try not to ponder too much! Except for the dramatic murders that move plots forward on our favorite shows, we work to keep the reality of death hidden away.

People do not usually die at home but in hospitals and "facilities." Bodies are made presentable and displayed in funeral homes. How very different from one hundred years ago. My grandfather told stories about his aunts and uncles passing away at home, cared for in those final days by the entire family. Following death, their caskets would lie in the front room of the family home so that neighbors and friends could visit and pay their respects. Back then, church members were as likely to prepare the deceased for burial as a paid professional. Of course, my grandfather also lived on a farm and raised animals for food. Death was much more a part of the fabric of his life than a part of mine. My meat comes in tidy foam and cellophane packages. Most of us do not witness the sacrifices which sustain our way of life.

I am not advocating huge social changes, only pointing out that we do not have a particularly "natural" approach to death. Helmut Thielicke, a twentieth century theologian, noted that modern culture treats death the way the Victorian era dealt with sexuality. We romanticize it, deal with it publicly when we must, push its emotional baggage down deep within us, and try not to talk about it in polite conversation.

How very different from the way scripture approaches death! All four gospels make the death and resurrection of Jesus the climax of the story.

"On the first day of the week, very early in the morning, the women took the spices they had prepared and went to the tomb. They found the stone rolled away from the tomb, but when they entered, they did not find the body of the Lord Jesus. While they were wondering about this, suddenly two men in clothes that gleamed like lightning stood beside them. In their fright the women bowed down with their faces to the ground, but the men said to them, 'Why do you look for the living among the dead? He is not here; he has risen! Remember how he told you, while he was still with you in Galilee: "The Son of Man must be delivered over to the hands of sinners, be crucified and on the third day be raised again."' Then they remembered his words." (Luke 24:1-8)

Followers of Jesus are taught to look death right between the eyes and accept its reality. We hold worship services on Good Friday, the day Jesus was crucified so we can feel the weight of his death and the power of his love. We try not to turn away from the pain of grieving, but acknowledge its burden. Then, and only then, can we appreciate the Easter morning celebration: "Christ is risen! Christ is risen indeed!" Jesus Christ conquered death. That is the foundation for our faith. *"'Where, O death, is your victory? Where, O death, is your sting?' The sting of death is sin, and the power of sin is the law. But thanks be to God! He gives us the victory through our Lord Jesus Christ."* (1 Corinthians 15:55-57)

Easter is God's public declaration that Jesus' teachings are correct. Light is stronger than darkness. Sin and death do not have the final word. In Christ, there is no such thing as a hopeless situation. Whether we are facing death or another circumstance that feels hopeless, the promise of scripture is that if we open ourselves to the presence of the Holy Spirit and do our best to follow the path forged by Jesus, God is with us. God will not abandon us.

Never Alone

Following Jesus and believing in the coming resurrection is not a guarantee that we will never face life challenges. In fact, Christ promises that we will! However, it also means that we will never have to face those challenges alone. We have been invited to participate in a community of faith, and we are promised God's Spirit as companion on the journey. The Gospel According to John makes this connection clear for us. Immediately following the resurrected Christ's appearance to Mary Magdalene, he visits the disciples. *"On the evening of that first day of the week, when the disciples were together, with the doors locked for fear of the Jewish leaders, Jesus came and stood among them and said, 'Peace be with you!' After he said this, he showed them his hands and side. The disciples were overjoyed when they saw the Lord. Again Jesus said, 'Peace be with you! As the Father has sent me, I am sending you.' And with that he breathed on them and said, 'Receive the Holy Spirit.'"* (John 20:19-22)

For his anxious followers, Jesus brings peace and the Holy Spirit. These two gifts are interdependent and define what it means to be a hope-filled people. The peace of Christ does not mean the disciples of Jesus will not suffer pain as they go forth. Jesus is sending them into a broken world. Not everyone will be pleased to hear their message of a true Lord that brings new life and hope in the face of death because not everyone is willing to follow God's desires for themselves or creation. But for those who welcome God's Spirit and seek to follow the way of life Jesus teaches, there is a powerful underlying peace in knowing that we are not alone. The power of God that raised Jesus Christ from the dead is at work in our lives (Ephesians 1:17-23).

God's Spirit is with us on our journey through this world. The Spirit reminds us of what God has accomplished for us in the past, filling us with a confident expectation that God's promises for our future will be fulfilled, even in the face of death. In Christ, death is not a sign of hopelessness; it is a deeper encounter with the Creator who desires to bring abundance and life (John 10:10). As "A Statement of Faith of the United Church of Canada" states: "In life, in death, in life beyond death, God is with us. We are not alone. Thanks be to God."

A Spiritual Practice

The path to experiencing the presence of the Holy Spirit and the peace of Christ is found in communal worship. All of the spiritual practices we have discussed so far could be categorized under the heading "individual worship." Obviously these are valuable and worthy of our time. However, worship that is offered to God as a member of the Body of Christ is life-changing.

Be careful. Do not confuse worship with entertainment or merely attending a church. Worship is not something you watch; it is a service you offer to God. It is the act of honoring God by offering your whole self in reverence and submission. Too many people come to a worship service in order to enjoy the music offered, learn something new, or feel good about themselves. It is certainly nice when those things take place, but they have nothing to do with the act of worship in its strictest sense. The music, scriptures, prayer, message, etc. are intended to create an atmosphere conducive to encountering God. Whether or not we have such a personal encounter depends on how open to God's Spirit we are in that moment.

Worship occurs when we authentically respond to the presence of God. When we are aware of God's presence and take seriously that we stand before our Lord, we become honest about our thoughts, actions, achievements, failures, desires, and future. This experience takes many different forms, depending on what we bring into the encounter. One person may need to confess sin, another dance with joy, and a third sit quietly listening for the Spirit to speak. We need to recognize that what Soren Kierkegaard said is true. "Worship isn't God's show. God is the audience. God's watching. The congregation, they are the actors in this drama. Worship is their show. And the minister is just reminding the people of their forgotten lines."

We should attempt to have an authentic encounter whenever we pray, meditate, read scripture, etc. Yet, when we worship God within a community of faith we experience, encouragement and conviction. Our voices mingle together in praise and prayer. We are reminded that others need our support and compassion as much as we need theirs. It is as Jesus promised, *"For where two or three gather in my name, there am I with them."* (Matthew 18:20)

1) Find a community of faith where worship is taken seriously. The leaders of worship should offer their best to God, but avoid those who tend toward entertaining the congregation.

2) Prepare yourself to worship God before you arrive. Make the decision ahead of time to focus on God more than the people around you. Consider what will help you do that: sitting away from friends and family or with them; spending time in prayer before the service or fellowshipping with others; etc. Respect that others may have a different way than you of readying themselves for worship.

3) Participate, do not spectate. When scripture is read, listen with the knowledge that God may use the words to communicate to you personally or to the congregation as a whole. When instrumental music is played, allow it to guide your thoughts and prayers. When songs are offered, allow their words to become your prayer or a message from God to you. When the sermon is proclaimed, recognize when the preacher's words speak for the congregation to God and when they speak for God, through the words of scripture, to the

congregation. Clap your hands, if that is a comfortable way for you to praise God. Or sit quietly. Engage. Be aware.

Be open to the Holy Spirit moving. Be honest with God about your feelings and emotions or your need for forgiveness, healing, or guidance. Remember that God is with you. Allow that presence to guide you in the way of peace.

"Now may the Lord of peace himself give you peace at all times and in every way. The Lord be with all of you." (2 Thessalonians 3:16)

Bibliography

Introduction - The Idea

Stossel, Scott. *My Age of Anxiety: Fear, Hope, Dread, and the Search for Peace of Mind.* New York: Alfred A. Knopf, January 7, 2014.

Chapter One - Focus on Good News

http://www.npr.org. Despite Grim Media Reports Crime Rates Are Actually Down. National Public Radio, December 23, 2015.

http://www.hsrgroup.org/. The Human Security Report Project, March 3, 2014.

http://www.slate.com. The World Is Not Falling Apart. Slate, December 22, 2014.

http://www.economist.com. Where Have All The Burglars Gone?, July 20, 2013.

http://www.economist.com. The Curious Case Of the Fall In Crime, July 20, 2013.

http://data.unicef.org/child-mortality/under-five.html. UNICEF, October, 2015.

http://www.healthdata.org. Death Rates Decline. IHME, 2013.

Chapter Two - Learn Who You Are

http://www.nytimes.com. The Anxious Americans. New York Times, July 18, 2015.

http://bigthink.com. How America Became The World's Most Anxious Nation.

Chapter Three - Stay Connected

http://www.latinospost.com. Social Media Pressure May Cause Anxiety, Depression on Teens – Study. Latinos Post, September 13, 2015.

http://www.alternet.org. How Our Society Breeds Anxiety, Depression, and Dysfunction,
August 21, 2013.

http://www.today.com. American Anxiety. NBC News, August 20, 2012.

http://www.slate.com. It's Not The Job Market, January 31, 2011.

https://www.psychologytoday.com. Why American Culture Is Plagued By Anxiety.
L. Kevin Chapman, January 29, 2012.

http://www.theguardian.com. Now The Good News. Steven Pinker, September 11, 2015.

Chapter Four - Be Part of Something Bigger

http://spectator.org. The Loneliness of American Society. May 18, 2014.

http://www.salon.com. How Our Society Breeds Anxiety. August, 26, 2013.

http://happierhuman.wpengine.netdna-cdn.com/wp-content/uploads/2014/06/P13.-Social-Isolation-in-America-Changes-in-Core-Discussion-Networks-over-Two-Decades.pdf. Social Isolation In America. ASR, June 30, 2010.

https://today.duke.edu. Americans Have Fewer Friends. Duke June, 2006.

Chapter Six - Learn to Lament and Celebrate

http://www.scientificamerican.com. Negative Emotions Are Key To Well Being. Rodriguez, May 1, 2013.

https://www.psychologytoday.com. Emotional Acceptance: Why Feeling Bad Is Good. September 8, 2010.

Chapter Seven- Find Light in the Darkness

http://well.blogs.nytimes.com. The Midlife Crisis Goes Global. New York Times, January, 30, 2008.

http://psychcentral.com. The 9 Types Of Hopelessness. October 14, 2009.

About the Author

Mark Flynn is the Senior Pastor of Christ United Methodist Church in Chattanooga. His wife, Annette, is also an ordained United Methodist Church pastor. They have two daughters, a son-in-law, and four grandchildren. He enjoys chess, Led Zeppelin, and backpacking on the Appalachian Trail. His idea of a perfect date with Annette includes hot buffalo wings, a cold beverage, and lots of laughter.